WE ALMOST DISAPPEAR

BOOKS BY DAVID BOTTOMS

POETRY

We Almost Disappear
Waltzing through the Endtime
Oglethorpe's Dream
Vagrant Grace
Armored Hearts: Selected and New Poems
Under the Vulture-Tree
In a U-Haul North of Damascus
Shooting Rats at the Bibb County Dump
Jamming with the Band at the VFW (limited edition)

NOVELS

Easter Weekend
Any Cold Jordan

PROSE/INTERVIEWS

The Onion's Dark Core:
A Little Book of Poetry Talk

ANTHOLOGY

The Morrow Anthology of Younger American Poets
(co-editor)

DAVID BOTTOMS

WE ALMOST DISAPPEAR

COPPER CANYON PRESS

PORT TOWNSEND, WASHINGTON

Printed in the United States of America
Cover art: Sally Mann, *Untitled,* c. 1998, Silver Gelatin Print
Image Size: 18 x 23 inches; Paper Size: 20 x 24 inches
© 1998 Sally Mann
Courtesy of the Artist

Copper Canyon Press is in residence at Fort Worden State Park in Port
Townsend, Washington, under the auspices of Centrum. Centrum is a
gathering place for artists and creative thinkers from around the world,
students of all ages and backgrounds, and audiences seeking extraordinary
cultural enrichment.

LIBRARY OF CONGRESS CATALOGING-IN-PUBLICATION DATA
Bottoms, David.
We almost disappear / David Bottoms.
P. CM.
ISBN 978-1-55659-331-4 (PBK.)
I. TITLE.
PS3552.O819W42 2011
811'.54—DC22
                                2011014869

98765432 FIRST PRINTING

COPPER CANYON PRESS
Post Office Box 271
Port Townsend, Washington 98368
www.coppercanyonpress.org

Thanks to the editors of the following publications in which some of these poems first appeared: *AGNI, Alaska Quarterly Review, Atlanta Journal-Constitution, The Georgia Review, The Gettysburg Review, The Hopkins Review, The Kenyon Review, Narrative, New South, Pleiades, Ploughshares, Poetry, Poetry Ireland Review, Shenandoah, The Southern Review, TriQuarterly,* and *The Yale Review.*

"Romanticism I" (under the title "In Willingham Chapel") first appeared in *Gladly Learn, Gladly Teach,* edited by John Marson Dunaway.

"My Father's Left Hand" was reprinted in American Life in Poetry, edited by Ted Kooser.

"Montana Wedding Day," "A Walk to Sope Creek," "A Chat with My Father," and "My Father Adjusts His Hearing Aids" were featured online in *Poetry Daily.*

"Holidays and Sundays" was featured in *Verse Daily.*

Thanks to David Baker, Bob Hill, Jane Hill, Edward Hirsch, Dave Smith, and Ernest Suarez for helpful readings of these poems.

Thanks also to Eavan Boland and *Shenandoah* for awarding "First Woods" the 2007 James Boatwright Prize for Poetry.

And special thanks to Michael Wiegers and Copper Canyon Press.

for Kelly and Rachel,
patience, faith, love

CONTENTS

1

2

WE ALMOST DISAPPEAR

1

And whoever remembers his childhood best
is the winner,
if there are any winners.
Yehuda Amichai

Maybe if I were a child again...
or could go crazy.
Miklós Radnóti

First Woods

Bump and jostle, the road falling fast into rut, ditch, washout,
pines cuffing the windows, and me in the cab
a constant bounce between my old man and my uncle
as we bring up the tail
of a caravan of trucks tumbling like a rockslide
leveling into splash and creek-bog,
then back-end swerve and up, and rear tires throwing mud
as my old man crunches gears in a field of orange light
where the sun falls in layers
through the splayed tops of pines...

and here we are on my uncle's place,
tailgates dropping, cages
swinging open, the meadow of brown grass crazy with scent,
until one bark rises, circles and leads,
and the whole pack swarms the woods.

Buzzards over the field, and crows, then a circus of bats,

but mostly I've kept the jar and pitch, a clearing of cut hay,
the moonlight rusting a tractor, and off
in the black woods, that thing I never saw, dragging
those frantic voices.

Violets

Little wallow of snuff pouching her lower lip, my grandmother spits
into a marble flower box
        and tilts a wide sprinkle from a rusted
        watering can.

Already this morning, August like a sweaty blanket grates the skin,
and the little African violets speckling
the narrow porch boxes
        gore up purple in the heavy light.
1955, and my grandmother isn't old, though she stoops at the
    shoulders
and treads what she calls the shady side of the slope.
She shuffles from box to box, leaning over violets, spitting into the
    black silk
a clotted stream of tobacco juice.
              Hex? Nutrient?
Slayer of aphids and mealybugs?

Not then, but now, I think of her desperate faith in dirt,
the prudence of watering can, the balance
of light and shade.
        Her name was Lily, and she dreamed of flowers.
Little cousins of the dream flowers,
she called her violets. Other dreams she never shared.

She spat tobacco juice into her flower boxes
and wiped her mouth on her sleeve—
            a small mouth, wrinkled,
blackened around the edges like a wilting leaf.

Husks

On the hill above the pasture, the pines
are holding out again. Already the dog lots are matted with leaves,
the kudzu falling away from the chicken houses.

We walk to the fence and watch the horses grazing the brown pasture.
Their rusty coats, growing shaggy, ruffle along their shoulders
in the early wind.
                From the grocery bag
my grandmother takes the husks and slaps them against a post,
a rustle that lifts their ears, and I whistle like the wind
only a few weeks off.

My grandmother slaps the corn husks easy
against the post. She doesn't know what's withering inside her.
Only the horses show any urgency, only
their slow shifting of weight,
                    that loosening of shoulders
growing quicker and quicker,
as they close on those corn husks wagging in her hand,
those last green scraps blooming in her hand.

My Grandpa Builds an Airplane

Rattle and snarl. Wind scattering sawdust over the oak shade...

I never thought it would fly, though the wings looked good
and the slope of the tail.
It was too square in the nose, and the plywood wasn't all that thick.

No, I never thought it would fly. But something
in me... well, what did I know about flying? I was only five,
and what hadn't my grandpa built?
Houses, dog lots, chicken coops...

All I brought to the business was an itch. He brought a hammer
and a saw, a rule that wound out
of a metal case, a compass that turned a circle
into a five-pointed star.
But no matter how I twisted
those wooden knobs or kicked the floor
of the cockpit, that propeller
never turned. Not once, even in the wind.

I shook my head and watched him rack his tools.

He looked solid, he stood up straight, and it was years
until anyone would call him broken.
I twisted those knobs, I rocked those wings.
Still, I loved the man.
What did I care
if nothing he touched ever got off the ground?

Adios, Horses

The way the thing screamed,
the way it snorted in the barn, tossed its head and slung hot spit,
bucked, reared, kicked at the stall—hey, forget Trigger,
forget Silver, Champion, Topper, Scout.

My old man and the folks he worked for
thought a pony would hook me on horses, and someday, like him,
I'd parade them in shows
and line their tack rooms with ribbons and trophies.

Sure I loved the notion, the romance
of the genuine autographed Gene Autry saddle, the silver bit,
the embossed bridle.
                    I loved those cowboy guitars
and the sound of hooves clomping off toward the sunset.

But when my old man dragged that pony through the pasture,
when he dragged that bucking pony, snarling
and jerking at the bit, well...
                    He held the bridle
and swung me into the saddle,

and the pony shied and danced. It jitterbugged, dipped,
and my old man jerked the bit,
handed me the reins
and pushed away.

Then adios, Diablo. Adios, Loco.
Oh, Cisco! Oh, Pancho!

After the Stroke

By the time he'd hit eighty, he was something out of Ovid,
his long beak thin and hooked,
                          the fingers of one hand curled and stiff.
Still, he never flew. Only sat in his lawn chair by the highway,
waving a bum wing at passing cars.

I was a timid kid, easily spooked. And it seemed like touchy gods
were everywhere—in the horns
and roar of diesels, in thunder, wind, tree limbs thrashing
the windows at night.

I was ashamed to be afraid of my grandfather.
But the hair on his ears!
                     The cackle in his throat!
Then on his birthday, my mother coaxed me into the yard.
I carried the cake with the one tiny candle

and sat it on a towel in the shade.
I tried not to tremble,
but it felt like gods were everywhere—in the grimy clouds
smothering the pine tops, the chain saw
in Cantrell's woods—everywhere, everywhere,
and from the look of the man
in the lawn chair, he'd pissed one off.

A Slight Nod to Slick Pope

Who'd sashay the mowed field like a shitfaced drum major,
blessing hay bales with his VA hook,

who taught me, a kid, to match nickels in the barn loft
and kept my precious nickels when I lost,

who swilled down the pocket change Uncle Sam tossed him
for the arm he left at Anzio

and odd-jobbed around horses and hunting dogs,
cluttered yards and greasy windows,

who shot bull like a pro over the potbellied stove
in my grandpa's grocery, rattling off

whoppers over Slim Jims and jerky,
Cracker Jacks and pork rinds,

who hatched big dreams with big-eyed hicks
over Dr Peppers and salted peanuts,

who cackled back when he was laughed at, quaking
from chin to butchered knees:

the closest we came to poetry.

A Swipe of Slick's Hook

Eyes blackened, lip bleeding, he crossed the highway
in front of my grandfather's store,
                                        a glinting swipe of his nickel hook
warning off the one car passing. A blistering afternoon,
two-minute summer downpour, then the sun steaming the blacktop
      like a river,

and the way he staggered—one-stepping, flapping wings, dragging
his foot like a Holiness shuffle—it might have been the Jordan
and him some soul desperate for salvation,
or sympathy, or worse still, credit.

Easy enough to see he was plastered.
His wife had left again, or had simply left, I can't remember.
I was only fourteen,
and the heat alone would've made you dizzy.

Skinned eyes and cracked babble,
that VA hook flailing the air—of all the ragged pictures
of grief, I don't know why he'd shadow me,

though something, sure, about the feel of this house, this empty dark,
as though you were holding everything you loved
in a hand that had vanished.

We Take My Grandpa Fishing

Dusk already, and a few random croakers on the far bank.

My mother whips the flashlight around her feet—copperheads,
    moccasins,
who knows what else in these weeds.
But this is the time to fish, when dark blurs the woods,
and croakers tune up
along the smudged-out bank.

He scoots his lawn chair too close to the water and leans out
over the shallows. She's set down the rules,
she shakes her finger.

Wind at our backs, and his left hand whips the cane pole.
The tall weeds hiss, the black trees
rattle their scales. Heavy belches circle the pond,
and he perks an ear.

This is the time to fish, the wind stirring, the water cooling,
the dark swallowing the pond. Sure, he hates
the pole, but he can't manage a reel, not since the stroke,
not with his bum right hand.

He's not complaining, though,
not about the hand. It flops now on his bony leg, warty,
spotted, puffed like a frog on a root.

In Sunday School

No one ever knew the lesson.
Sunday after Sunday, we sat around a wobbly table

and listened to Mr. Reynolds twist a Southern Baptist slant
into a Bible story none of us had read.

Almost in high school and no one knew the meaning
of the widow's mite, or why the father of the prodigal son

killed the fatted calf. No one understood the parable
of the talents, or could even recite the Ten Commandments.

We were always as blank as the empty blackboard,
sniggering and cracking jokes,

until Mr. Reynolds, one morning, spun midverse
and threw his lesson book at Ricky Doehla.

He stared at his hand, stood, and left the room.
That may have been the morning we all grew up.

And having grown up eventually left home,
left Canton, left the church

to be gutted into a new city hall,
where the commandments that count

are the laws of the state,
though Jesus still lingers in the remodeled lobby—

trapped in stained glass—
breaking into baskets his fishes and loaves.

My Old Man's Saddle

Where were we going? I remember only the backward lunge
onto the road, and my mother shifting
into first, her soft face
graying as she whispered the news.

Sunlight glinted in the corner of the windshield, and oddly
the wipers flapped. But only twice
before I'd brushed it off. I was fourteen years old.

For days though the television, all three channels, showed
nothing but grainy news reports.
Then full coverage of the state funeral—
shock of coffin in gun carriage, seven white horses,
a black horse bearing
an empty saddle, stirrups reversed.

The widow's veiled and swollen face was far worse.

That evening I bagged some scraps
and walked to the barn.
                                    I tossed the corn husks into the stall,
then stood for a time at the tack room door, staring
at my old man's saddle,
an English saddle, draped across the saddle bar.

Holidays and Sundays

They'd settle in our living room, cross their legs—three or four uncles,
my old man. They'd stare at each other
and pull at their ears, while the women cleared the dishes.

Okay, maybe somebody would mention rain
and draw a nod from across the room, or a ball game
that had gone into extra innings,

but mostly there was silence, as though they'd all agreed
the world was beyond comment.

I grew up thinking this was how men behaved, holding
their thoughts close to their chests. A compliment, sure, at dinner—
the beans, the potatoes—but that was it.

Nobody fired off a joke, nobody lobbed a war story
over anybody's bow. Not the tiniest pinch
of philosophy, politics, theology.

Only that slow retreat into calculated silence,
which wasn't exactly boredom,
but more the silence you got at church or funerals,

which was the way you faced the sacred, or death,
or that inscrutable laughter from the kitchen.

Pinch-Hitting in the Playoffs

for Ernest Suarez

On the Cherokee High School baseball team, I didn't nab much
    respect
for being well-read. All the real jocks
got the at bats while I warmed the bench, knocking off
Russian novels.

For me that season was heat and dust and the bad light
of dugouts, and out in the glare
a constant scream off the infield, the outfield, the stands,
until one afternoon
in a frenzied croak the coach broke through the noise—
Grab a bat! Grab a bat!

It was nothing as dramatic as a tied ball game
or even a squeaker we might pull out—
only a chance to take a swing
in a game we had no chance of winning.

I don't even recall the score, only the chatter,
the haze, the heat, the dust
like cannon smoke drifting off the infield,
then the coach against the dugout fence,
shooting crazy signs with his hand—cap, nose, eye,
cap, nose, eye.

And all I could think
was Lev Nikolaevich, don't let Prince Andrei die.

The Undertaker's Words

...invoke the inadequacy of the human tongue.
Czesław Miłosz

When the telephone shrieks in the middle of the night, nothing good.

I learned this early, listening to my old man stumble
through the dazed hall. He'd manage *hello*
or something close,
                        then that long silence of detail as he'd try to clear
                        his fog.

No, when the telephone rings in the middle of the night, well...

And him zoned-out and beat, having worked all day
and half the night before,
                        and always somebody at a bedside, distraught,
a wife who won't let go of a hand, or a daughter
who's slept in the same dress for days. Or worse still a father staring
at nothing, lost in the emptiness of a wall.

He'd hit the bathroom, muttering *What to say, what to say?*
then lean over the sink, splash water
on his face.
                  Over and over, cold water on his face,
and him beat and punchy, trying to wake up the heart,
wake up the brain, roust out a word...
a few tired words.

2

nothing is ever entirely
right in the lives of those who love each other.

Eavan Boland

Montana Wedding Day

Three fat trout on my wedding day, two cutthroats
and a rainbow from the Thompson River.

All morning I flicked spoons into the riffles
and three trout leapt the rocks to follow them into my hands.

Never mind the cutthroats were undersized
and illegal, never mind I had no license,

I carried my luck to a flat rock jutting the bend
and, one by one, scraped their bright guts into the river.

I built a little fire of charcoal and lay back on the shelf—
wheat bread, corn chips, soda,

and grilled trout savored all the way down
to the needles of their spines.

A fish hawk fell from a dead tree and thrashed the river,
clawing up another trout. I thought, sure,

to have tumbled so far
and finally to have reached a beginning.

I was gorged and grateful. I gathered my tackle,
bagged my trash, scattered bones and scraps,

then lay back for an hour in hemlock shade,
watching a fisheye glaze to a pearl.

A Walk with Rachel

Up and down Paper Mill, in the dwindling light,
small American flags bloom from gates and mailboxes. We're pondering
    evil,
my daughter and I,
                    and the spooky history of hatred.
The Devil's shoes don't creak, she says,
                            a proverb she's heard from her
                            granny.

At ten she's letting her hair grow, and diligently keeping a journal.

Later, she too may puzzle out inadequately
                            the significance of this
                            moment—

but no words yet to chill the jittery voice,
only these few crickets cranking up in the shrubbery, the whine
of a motorbike a mile away.

We shuffle quietly to the end of the street.

Now the full confusion of darkness,
and our old sidekick, the North Star, dim over the cul-de-sac—
silent, but there.

My Daughter Works the Heavy Bag

A bow to the instructor,
then fighting stance, and the only girl in karate class faces the heavy bag.
Small for fifth grade—*willowlike,* says her mother—
sweaty hair tangled like blown willow branches.

The boys try to ignore her. They fidget against the wall, smirk,
practice their routine of huff and feint.
                                        Circle, barks the instructor,
jab, circle, kick, and the black bag wobbles on its chain.

Again and again, the bony jewels of her fist
                                        jab out in glistening precision,
her flawless legs remember *arabesque* and *glissade.*
Kick, jab, kick, and the bag coughs rhythmically from its gut.

The boys fidget and wait—
then a whisper somewhere, a laugh, a jeer.

She circles the bag—*jab, jab, jab*—flushed, jaw set, huffing
with her punches, huffing with her kicks, circles
to her left and glares.
                        But only at the bag—alone, in herself,
to her own time, in her own rhythm, honing her blocks
and feints, her solitary dance,
having mastered already the first move of self-defense.

A Blessing, Late

Up from the creek behind the cul-de-sac, it skulked
through tree line and subdivided shadows, static of crickets
and trembling leaves, following blood
and scent of meat
to leap my backyard fence.

And if I'd tried the window a good second sooner
or hadn't bumped my knee against the blind,
I might have caught it edged
against the shrubbery,
and met it, for a moment, eye to solid eye,
but as it occurred only that gray and long-legged blur
ghosting into the trees.

And I remembered a girl across our street, taping
a poster to a Stop sign. For weeks
pets had been vanishing, the Persian next door, a calico,
even the fat Pomeranian
that prissed behind
my neighbor's invisible fence.

But I kept staring over my blackened shrubs
and wheelbarrow, my stacked bales
of pine-straw, into the dark between the trees, trying
to bring back that glimpse
and trembling, that nervy blur
that suffered no need
for my dog chow, my water bowl,
or my blessing.

Dream of the Dusty Attic

Dusty heat, stale air rising out of old lumber, constant eerie twilight
wallowing like toxic fog through the vents...

Strange to climb

into the underworld, to hang on the edge of a trapdoor,
letting eyes adjust.

But this is the dream of first things, of boyhood.
Of old stories, of climbing
through a cluttered closet into the attic of a lost house.

A stroller with rusted spokes, a beach ball, deflated,
crushed hatbox, a woman's boot,

but sure enough, piled farther back,

those books I keep coming back for and can never quite reach,
four or five picture books, waterlogged, faded.

I stretch out a heavy arm...

then that familiar wave of loss, of stale air rising, attic blurring
and rocking, and the books sliding farther away...

How odd, though, and sweet the payback,

the way they blend with rafters and twilight into one felt story—
one dim beginning, one dark ending—

the sour mouth

of the whale, the vaporous cave, the splintered ribs
of that stifling wooden horse.

Little Dream of Spilt Coffee

for Kelly

Yipes, I thought, *don't put that cup on the floor...*
But you'd set it already on the Oriental rug

to pat down the pillows on the sofa,
and of course, when you turned, you caught it with your heel.

My heart, wobbly for days, tipped again
until I saw the cup had turned over but the coffee hadn't spilled—

no, the coffee had stayed in the cup, no mess, no stain,
the shade-grown coffee from Costa Rica still inside the cup,

inexplicable as mysticism, or love, as though the laws of nature
had shifted to accommodate our mistakes.

It was our red cup, I remember, covered with moons
and caribou, and when I picked it up

and held it between us, you steadied it in both hands,
then lifted it to your lips.

Little Dream of Fishing

Half the stars trembled on the water, half in the black sky, and the
    moon
like a silver hook,
                dangled low over the pines.
A small wind nudged our boat toward the middle of the lake,
and I cast and cast without a decent strike.
You lay back half-asleep, letting a wad of dead worms drift behind us.
The point, in your philosophy, wasn't the fishing.

Then the wind picked up with a sense of peril. You know—big lake,
    small boat.
In the dream I felt this was all a compensation—I'd been suffering
from a silly hope—and just as we drifted over the deepest water,
my rod bent hard.

But I jerked, you jerked, and the boat shook the stars.

A Cello Bird

On the patio my daughter
is practicing her cello. She's dragged her chair near the edge of the
     grass,
where a patch of moonlight
                         borders the woolly trees.
If she looks straight up, she can catch a few stars.
Straight ahead, the smudged dark.

She leans forward, shoulders curled, and the shadows
streaking the patio blend girl
and cello into one clumsy bird—bent neck, hooked beak, one wing
     flapping.

Before long the trees sing back.

When I was a boy I, too, wanted to become a bird
and, day after day,
                    whistled through the scrub woods behind our
                    house.

But the crows mocked me, and the cardinals ignored me,
and the sparrows, thrashers, towhees, jays.

Who knows how she charms those tiny voices out of the dark
and keeps them singing
in the yard? Who knows how far they travel?
                         Or where
she's planning to go
all dressed up in that plumage of shadow.

Bull Elk, Midwinter

Why so low today? Your hollow cheeks, labored smile...
even worse, it seems, than last night.
Listen ... high, high up in the mountains of Montana
a majestic elk parades the slopes.

Huge and agile, he tosses a rack like two small oaks, antlers
no mountain lion would ever chance. Floating
above a cliff, decoding
the wind, he's muscle and nerve at the ready.

Heavy clouds, like a winter coat, tumble his back,
and he feels how, beyond
the far ridges, blown rain slakes into ice.
He knows on which slopes the tree bark is most tender,

and knows also the roads twisting like narrow rivers,
the clumsy trucks of hunters.
Maybe he even remembers our glasses
flinging sparks behind a foggy windshield.

Come away from the window now, please,
from the concrete, the dirty slush.
Are those tears? Listen ... high up in the peaks of Montana
a majestic elk parades the slopes.

Walking a Battlefield: A Love Story

for Kelly

Fog most always suggests the otherworldly.

Forget I said that,
                    or mark it off to horror flicks and adolescent
                    mysticism.
Nevertheless, after a cool rain, in the evening,
when mist gathers its loose foot soldiers in the fields
below Kennesaw,
                    you can easily imagine or even believe you hear
boots tramping down brush along the skirt
of the mountain.

Now, at sixty, I crave these walks,
where sometimes in the evening, along these trails,
throaty voices croak up for us,
                    like a hummed spiritual,
or an altar moan, or a night wind through the weedy graveyard
of a B movie,
                    and we nerve-up just enough
to walk out toward them, along those foggy earthworks,
into those dips, those wallows,
where one hand takes another as we almost disappear.

A Walk to Sope Creek

Sometimes when I've made the mistake of anger, which sometimes
breeds the mistake of cruelty, I walk

down the rocky slope above the ruined mill on Sope Creek
where sweet gum and hickory weave sunlight

into gauzy screens. And sometimes when I've made the mistake
of cruelty, which always breeds grief,

I remember how, years ago, my uncle led me, a boy,
into a thicket of pines and taught me to kneel

beside a white stone, the way a man had taught him, a boy,
to pray behind a clapboard church.

Sometimes when my heart is as dark as a stone, I weave
between trees above that crumbling mill

and stumble through those threaded screens of light,
the way an anger must fall

through many stages of remorse.
Any rock, he allowed, can be an altar.

Striped Bangle on Sope Creek

I pushed back the branch
                    and it fell like a bracelet across my arm—
a scarlet king or a coral, but panic like beauty
stunned me, and I couldn't remember which pattern was deadly,
the yellow bands against the red,
                         or the red against the black...

then a jolt in my head and a blur, and an old poem
opened onto a grave
where gray bones tangled like roots
and a bracelet of black hair circled a wrist bone.
I stood on that path
and felt down my own bones a thrill I couldn't account for,
like my hand paralyzed in the air
or the shadows of the trees having crossed the path...

Wind startled the dogwoods, and my arm shook, and shook again,
until the thing wrapped around it
tumbled onto a rock.
Then an odd thought came—black hair or bright?—

as the snake crawled off into leafy shadows, sluggish,
undisturbed, nudging
its black nose through the scrub.

3

*Once we have understood we are nothing, the object
of all our efforts is to become nothing.*

Simone Weil

Love at the Sunshine Club

Macon, Georgia, 1970

Bloody smear across the moon
and I'm pondering again the sucker punch that decked me at the
    Shine—
Forsyth Street, forty years ago.
Two bikers, the bartender, me, and to light the fuse
a skinny girl in skintight blue jeans
                                  casually humping the jukebox.

I'd just turned to see who was screaming—when bam,
a flash of head-stars!
                 Blood in gushes
and a delicate haze screening the dingy lightbulb.
The floor tilted and rolled back,
a bar stool hit the wall, then
circling above me those raw eyes flushed with booze...

Tonight in Macon, only a sober and lonely tedium—
a bruised moon we've made
too much of, a few icy stars drifting
across the interstate.

But as long as I remember that wrenched and scalded face,
those shoulders trembling
like a wet dog, that spittle and sweat,
that red fist choking a beer can, how could I ever stop
believing in love?

Bluesman Home from a
Cherry Street Bar

A stumble into the dark...

                  stink of rotten floor, cigars, dim lilac
                  cologne.
His match finds a candle, and he lights three more,
sets them among clutter of mantel and table, a rubble of ivories
that once keyed an organ.

                  Posters of bluesmen wilt
on the walls—Lonnie Johnson, Johnny Shines, Bukka White.
For years they've moaned about women and work.

Two weeks of ditching means
bucks in his pocket now, but not enough to turn the lights back on.
Guitar in a corner, untouched for months,

                  and his blistered hands
are a lesson in regret. The chair sags deeper with his weight.

A sudsy light seeps through the curtains and a sudden need for air.
He stands and clutches the mantel, wobbles his way
to the porch.

                In Tattnall Square the usual gangsters
skulk under streetlights, shaking their bags like little bells.
He shoves back the screen and catches a breath.
The oak shadow deepens in the rocky yard.
He leans against the railing, he glares—as though it were a hole
he'd just paused from digging.

Under *The Blue Window*

Pardon, pardon...
              and we clutch our headphones, soft-shoeing
the waxed hardwood, craning, elbowing politely.

Then a noise, a rustle,
and the flock waddles in, kindergarten or first grade, like pigeons
in a cathedral, fluttering under the pictures, under
their teacher's *hush, hush...*

I edge past a fishbowl, and shy toward a corner, giving space.
An old gent scowls over his glasses, while a woman
in a red beret comforts
the frazzled muzzle of her fur.
                Notice, she says, *how the wall*
with the window creates a contiguity
between the natural world and the human room...

Most of the kids scuffle, squirm, but a few stray into the breeze
of guiding arms
           and land at the ledge of Matisse's window.

Almost a quiet before language comes—*lamp, tree, flower*—
and a child sits down
and crosses his legs, and another. A scuffle, a joke,
then a small girl in hearing aids
              lies back on the floor,
as though she were home in the silence of her bed,
gazing through her window at twilight.

A Beginning

In a green-shingled house off Highway 5
just south of Canton, Georgia, a boy sits on a throw rug in the corner
of his room. He's writing a tall tale, an assignment

for school. Frustrated and dull, he's panicked by the blank page,
until an older cousin, who'll
die soon in a war, conjures up a rodeo,

a bronc, and a cowboy bucked over the moon.
The cowboy circles a couple
of planets, then slides back to Earth on the Milky Way,

and the boy, who's jealous of his cousin, ponders
the imagination, a thing
that makes the pencil tremble in his hand.

Who, though, could've imagined that story would live so long—
the house torn down
and paved over, that cousin dreamless under a pink stone—

or that one swatch of stars on a clear night
would still look pale and slick
as cow's milk, and a blank page, even now, make me panic?

Romanticism I

for Ben Griffith

Old crone of a building sagging into its bricks, and a classroom
    dangling
off a creaking stairway.
                The desks creaked, too, the floor complained.
The crippled lectern tottered on its crutch. An old room, sure,
but not entirely dead,
each brittle window enlivening a yellowed page.

Wordsworth was there, and Dorothy, Coleridge with his tragic teeth,
Peacock and Lamb, Godwin
spouting sedition,
             portly Mr. Blake in the attic with his angels...

A quiet man spoke, and something woke up in my heart.
Gradually, the shy world wanted to talk.

But that was a long while ago,
                and other than gratitude
so little survives the world's chronic revision—a boss line, maybe,
from a poem you've forgotten, a penny
you picked up in an alley
for luck,
      a voice that blessed you in passing.

Learning to Become Nothing

for Carl Hays

Drizzle this morning,
but a cool glare in the brain, and I'm staggering again down Cherry
  Street
toward that cratered-out joint on Broadway
where one happy night, eons ago, I cut a rug with a hopped-up
  redhead.

Nothing came of that, Carl, except a few short hours of inexplicable
  joy,
so that each bad tooth in her gorgeous smile
                                        hardened into a little gem
                                        of memory.

Gems, Carl, gems. And this whole street paved with them—
    Otis Redding
strutting into your jewelry store, a sunburst off
the cracked face of his watch,
                        or that saintly Pearly Brown, blind as
                        the future,
pounding the sidewalk, slashing out a sermon on his National Steel.
God love a cheerful giver, Carl.

Yes, sir. His sign caught the whole shebang—
and now that we're learning to become nothing, we have to learn
to give it all away—every radiance,
every gem—
        cheerful, as you say, being the enigma.

My Poetry Professor's Ashes

remembering Lem Norrell

All those rhetorical contraptions of the metaphysicals
prying us loose from the world!
                              And those licentious exhortations to
                              squeeze the day!
Something about the Anglican burial
brought those back, and with them your voice rousing those metaphors
        off the page.
It's not like I didn't get a heads-up, right?

But I'd never seen a man's ashes, the human dust, fine, gray,
and when the priest upended the urn
and shook yours into the grass, I thought how much they looked like
        chalk dust,
like a lifetime of notes erased from a blackboard,
which seemed right enough
                              given what we are and what words come to.

4

*But what it is all about exactly I could no more say, at
the present moment, than take up my bed and walk.*

Samuel Beckett

...death has sent me its loneliness first.

Nazim Hikmet

Old Man and Neighborhood Hawk

Vague silhouette, like an idea
forming, then a shiver on the pine branch and the hawk takes shape.

It props against twilight to scrutinize the yard, the hedges
and flower beds smudged into gray pools.

My old man, elbow on his walker, stares from a kitchen chair.

The hawk rolls his head, probes hedge, patio, monkey grass,
rhododendrons heavy with black blossoms, trellis of roses.

The old man noses the window, his caught breath clouding the pane.

Something has grabbed an eye, some old impulse
trembling down the nerves. On the bar of the walker his hand
        trembles.

Then a dive from the branch, a bursting under brush,
and up the hawk rises on wing-slashes, pine-straw, flurry of leaves—

over lawn, fence, street, dragging through streetlight
something pale and squirming—

and my old man's hand flapping toward the window
falls again to his knee.

An Old Man Finds a Bench

The old undertaker, you'd hardly know him,
flops down on an empty park bench. He slouches back and sighs.

His walnut cane drops against a knee. Gently, in a way
you wouldn't recognize, say like a sunflower

on a weak stem, his smooth head bobs,
and blossoms of dogwoods roll across his glasses.

His suit is the color of smog. Way too hot for an April morning,
and his wife, that genuine small-town saint,

dabs a crushed hankie at the corner of his mouth.
Her face and hair are a thin

cream of wheat. In the shadows she almost isn't there.
Her eyes slide down to his crotch and away...

Beyond the rusted slide a little procession of pigeons
hardly spooks for the First Baptist crowd,

but the woman, my mother, spiffy and neat, leans up
from the bench to straighten her blouse.

She glances again at his fly yawning slack
on the tail of his shirt. All those dark-suited years,

those decades of starch and decorum, and his fly
hangs slack on the tail of his shirt.

And one sock is brown, the other sock black.

My Mother's Abscess

The receptionist, in her marbled booth, jabs a pink nail into the
    phone.
All day, maybe, she hasn't noticed the potted ficus
between the revolving doors.

The potted ficus! Maybe no one has noticed but me
with my brown-bagged Dewar's and my fat Russian novel, on my way
to the second-floor waiting room
where, a few rooms down, surgeons are slicing a loop
from my mother's colon.

A snake in the ficus tree? Sure, as though it had slithered
out of some patient's dream, a red snake curled
like a bowel around the ficus, little red snake like something
out of a trick shop, curled
around the skinny trunk of the ficus.

When I was a kid I saw omens everywhere—a crow on the mailbox,
a black cat at a ball game, that evil number
turning up on Fridays...
                    I scratch my beard.
Upstairs my mother lies drugged, beyond dreams, beyond signs,
and here I'm spooked by the tiniest snake?

A few leaves tremble, the body loops. The lewd head rises
like a little chip off the original nightmare.

My Old Man Loves My Truck

Sometimes when I've driven the twenty-four miles
to buy a few groceries or change a light,

my old man leans on his walker in the doorway of the kitchen
and gazes across the carport at my truck.

And sometimes when the trembling is too much,
he edges his walker over the stoop and inches onto the driveway.

My old man loves my truck. It has all the right dents and scratches,
just the proper amount of rust.

He'll inch around the fenders, checking out the bed and hitch,
he'll ask to pop the hood.

And sometimes when my old man studies the cab, you can hear
in his pocket the empty rattle of keys.

Then his smile goes slack, his jaw flexes.
And soon that nervous rattle of walker, that rattle of bones

as he plows around the fenders at double-speed, checking
the panels, checking the spare,

as though every loss, every letdown, might be cleared up
by thumbing a scratch or kicking a tire.

My Old Man Loves Fried Okra

My old man's tired. He tries to follow the small talk of the woman
who's brought dinner, but his head nods toward his chest.

My old man won't say so, but he's beat, sapped, worn-out.
He tries to track the talk of the woman from his church,

but her words fall out of the air like sick birds,
and his eyelids grow heavy, and his head nods toward his chest.

This woman, this kind woman from Heritage Baptist,
has brought fried chicken, potatoes, a bowl of fried okra.

My old man loves fried okra—the smell of it, the taste of it,
the slight crunch between the teeth.

He eats it at lunchtime, at dinner. Hot from the pan,
cold from the fridge. He eats it with his fingers, like popcorn.

But his eyelids droop again and his head drops slowly
until his elbow slips off the arm of his chair.

This is what frightens me. How can he be too tired for thanks,
too tired to lift his head for the one simple word

he'd want to say? How can he be too tired for okra?

My Father's Garbage Can

My old man rings me on my cell. The garbage can is beside the road
and needs to be rolled back into the carport.

I scratch my head at the urgency in his voice.

The garbage can is sitting empty beside the road—
it needs to be rolled back into the carport.

How to say, how to say to my father, I can't drive fifty miles
to wheel his garbage can down the driveway?

But I know this isn't my old man asking. His voice, sure,
his gargle and rasp, but not my old man asking.

He knows the miles and the afternoon traffic,
how the big trucks clot the interstate.

His gargle, yes, his rasp and stutter, but not my father.
He knows the miles, he knows the traffic.

This is loneliness, the loose tongue of loneliness
nagging by the window

where he's sat all day with his elbow on his walker, staring
at the oak shade staining the yard

and the garbage can, empty, on the shoulder of the road.

A Chat with My Father

Sometimes when my old man tries to talk, his mind runs like a
    small boy
on a path through the woods.

You know the story. There's home to get to and it's getting late,
only a little light still slicing through the trees.

And the boy has walked the path so many times
he thinks he can do it in his sleep. But no. Some bird sounds off

way back in the woods, and he tries to ignore it, but it harps again,
and suddenly he's off the path, deeper and deeper

into the trees, wading the shadows, following the strangest
and most beautiful birdsong he's ever heard

until he crosses a stream and catches in the corner of his eye
a ruby as big as his fist, sure, a ruby or some rock

just as precious, and bends to pick it up when a wild dog...
no, not a dog, when a wolf barks across a gully,

and he's beating his way through brush and briar, trailing
those barks and howls already fading

in the distance. All the while the woods have grown dark,
and suddenly he looks across the table,

and you see in his eyes that he's lost.

Tedium

Every night my old man inches his walker across the kitchen floor—
to the cabinet for a glass, the sink for water.

And usually while he's leaning on the counter, or turning
from the sink with a glass in his hand,

the grandpa clock goes off in the hall. Eight chimes
like a gong falling down a well.

Then it's back through the den, around the sofa, down the hall—
glass wedged into the basket of his walker.

A hand on the bedpost for balance, the cautious lifting of the glass.
A shuffle then down the edge of the bed.

Finally, on the night table a glass of tepid water. A hell of a fuss,
he says, for what only makes him piss.

In the morning on the night table
an empty glass. And beside it a ring in the dust.

My Father Adjusts His Hearing Aids

Once again my old man has gutted his hearing aids.
On the table beside him, around the smallest blade of his pocketknife,

his hearing aids lie scattered like the scrutinized guts of bugs.
Somewhere in those parts—the coils, the disks,

the blue copper veins—somewhere in that chaos lies the riddle
of sound. Now in the dark kitchen he faces the window

where the first stars tremble in the branches of his oaks.
The house is as quiet as a broken watch.

He's pieced the clues—nothing will ever be
repaired again, nothing will ever work as it did. The dumb wind

says as much, and the needles raining in the yard.
The silence around his shoulder is my mother's arm.

My Father's Left Hand

Sometimes my old man's hand flutters over his knee, flaps in crazy
    circles,
and falls back to his leg.

Sometimes it leans for an hour on that bony ledge.

And sometimes when my old man tries to speak, his hand waggles in
    the air,
chasing a word, then perches again

on the bar of his walker or the arm of a chair.

Sometimes when evening closes down his window and rain blackens
into ice on the sill, it trembles like a sparrow in a storm.

Then full dark falls, and it trembles less, and less, until it's still.

5

I think we must be faithful to immortality, that other, slightly stronger name for life.

Boris Pasternak

In the end, everyone can do without fathers . . .

Salman Rushdie

On Cantrell's Pond

1

When I was a boy there was a pond behind our house

that eventually filled up with construction runoff—
a muddy pond of stunted catfish,
a mosquito hole, fetid,
wallow and paradise for copperheads, rats, moccasins, frogs,
and no few turtles that could take off your finger
with one surgical snap,

and at night, year-round, the stench rose thick
and seeped in waves
through the cracks in my window
where I'd curl like a snail at the foot of my bed, drifting
on deep breaths, far back.

I'm always dreaming my way back to water:

to a washed-out logging road
plunging to a river
where high buzzards recon the kudzued pines,
to a cove on a lake of monster gar, a tumbling creek
of killer rocks, a sky-black swamp choked with cypress
where I wade out knee-deep with my rod and rattle-bug
and never, in my exhaustion, outrun
the cottonmouth

that blesses my heel with its flower.

2

Why all of this middle-aged noise about getting back?

Though, for sure, in the mornings the leafy banks rustled
with birds—
                blue jays and cardinals, a towhee or two,
robins, thrashers, and dozens of barn sparrows
mobbing the dam where our neighbor, Mr. Cantrell,
crumbled biscuits for his fish,

and in the summer the forest of sunflowers
nodding in the wind at the edge
of his garden,
and the rosebushes crawling the bank
from the brush dam to his toolshed
all the way up to the chicken house collapsed
in a thicket of briars.

3

But out here, in middle age, or a mile or two beyond,
why all this hubbub about beginnings?
And why only one brief dream
of that pond
when now there's no other way back?

Or only a way back to kudzu and concrete,
to a Kentucky Fried Chicken where our house once stood,
a Taco Bell, a Pizza Hut,
an oily gas station, and across the highway
a Kmart strip mall, a Waffle House
where my grandpa once grazed horses.

In my dream the sky was a loose tumble of charcoal,
the silky trees bare and trembling.
Tall grass bit my ankles. I lifted my feet,
I had someplace to go. Then brush stalks shivered
as I stepped off the bank
and began to walk, carefully,
not on water but on the parched bed
of an empty pond
cobbled entirely with turtles.

Campfire in a Light Rain

1

Out here near the end, sometimes in my despair, I pack
a tent into the truck bed,
a few camping tools, firewood and kindling to save me some trouble,
and sandwiches, of course, and sardines,
water, soda, whatever,

and sometimes drive east to the Oconee River
to sit all night in a folding chair,
feeding sticks into a fire.

No radio, no cell phone, but a battery lantern for books.

Even at the end, I still need books, though the crickets are witness
that the story goes on a little while longer,
and the mallards skiing in
at twilight to bob under a sunken tree,
and the hermit owl far back in the woods
tossing out his eerie vibe,
and the tree frogs in the pines above the riverbank,
and the pines in the wind
above the riverbank.

2

My granny used to hear voices from her childhood,
the voices of schoolchildren
in Pickens County
long shoveled over in sanctified clay.

She never told anyone for fear of being shut away,
but took them as testimony
for that *land beyond the river, that Canaan of the saved.*

You tell me what the end looks like to you,
and I'll tell you about a river
under a night sky,
about the stars guttering out, one by one,
while a thicket of scrub pine darkens into a wall.

Does anyone have another idea?

3

The charred logs sizzle in the rain, and the chill off the river
bores like a dull blade into my knees.
By the time my old man
was my age he could hardly move without a groan.

I sit under the tent flap
and watch the mallards dabble around the fallen oak,
and a few wood ducks, an egret.
Three geese took off an hour ago, stringing out north
over the logging road, and everything now
is settling toward nightfall.

Whatever happened to the promise of wisdom?

The gray beard came, the cracked teeth,
the vanishing hair, the trembling hand,
but what became
of Solomon's crown?

I toss a few more sticks into the fire
and ponder my foolishness—

all of this time searching for purity
and never grasping the nature of ashes.

A Heron on the Oconee

1

Now on the Oconee, on this shallow elbow of quiet water,

the first moist sunlight seeps through the thicket,
and a heron streaked in feathered light strides out among the rocks.

Ruffled and muddy, it wobbles out into the river
and balances on sticks among the rocks,

utterly motionless among the rocks.

2

Near the end, the way my old man stared into the distance,

the way he leaned from his armchair
toward a window, elbow quivering on his walker,

and gazed through oak branches into a broken sky,
is the way this heron, ruffled, muddy,

stares downriver at the water rippling into the trees.

David Bottoms is the author of nine books of poems and two novels. Among the many awards he has received for his poetry are the Walt Whitman Award of the Academy of American Poets, an Ingram Merrill Award, an Award in Literature from the American Academy and Institute of Arts and Letters, the Levinson Prize and the Frederick Bock Prize from *Poetry*, and fellowships from the National Endowment for the Arts and the Guggenheim Foundation. He teaches at Georgia State University in Atlanta where he holds the John B. and Elena Diaz-Verson Amos Distinguished Chair in English Letters. He serves as Poet Laureate of Georgia.

 Since 1972, Copper Canyon Press has fostered the work of emerging, established, and world-renowned poets for an expanding audience. The Press thrives with the generous patronage of readers, writers, booksellers, librarians, teachers, students, and funders—everyone who shares the belief that poetry is vital to language and living.

Copper Canyon Press gratefully acknowledges board member

JIM WICKWIRE

for his many years of service to poetry and independent publishing.

MAJOR SUPPORT HAS BEEN PROVIDED BY:

THE **PAUL G. ALLEN**
FAMILY *foundation*

NATIONAL
ENDOWMENT
FOR THE ARTS

WASHINGTON STATE
ARTS COMMISSION

The Paul G. Allen Family Foundation

Amazon.com

Anonymous

Diana and Jay Broze

Beroz Ferrell & The Point, LLC

Golden Lasso, LLC

Gull Industries, Inc.
on behalf of William and Ruth True

Lannan Foundation

Rhoady and Jeanne Marie Lee

National Endowment for the Arts

Cynthia Lovelace Sears and Frank Buxton

Washington State Arts Commission

Charles and Barbara Wright

To learn more about underwriting
Copper Canyon Press titles, please call
360-385-4925 X103

The poems are set in Adobe Garamond Pro. The headings are set in Avenir. Book design and composition by Phil Kovacevich. Printed on archival-quality paper at McNaughton & Gunn, Inc.

The Chinese character for poetry is made up of two parts: "word" and "temple." It also serves as pressmark for Copper Canyon Press.